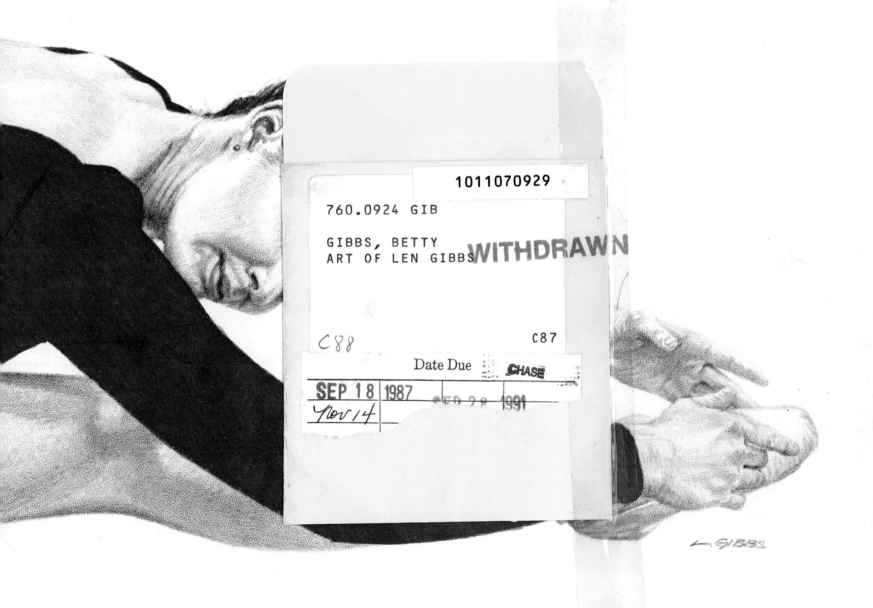

L. GIBBS

THE ART OF
LEN · GIBBS

Betty Gibbs

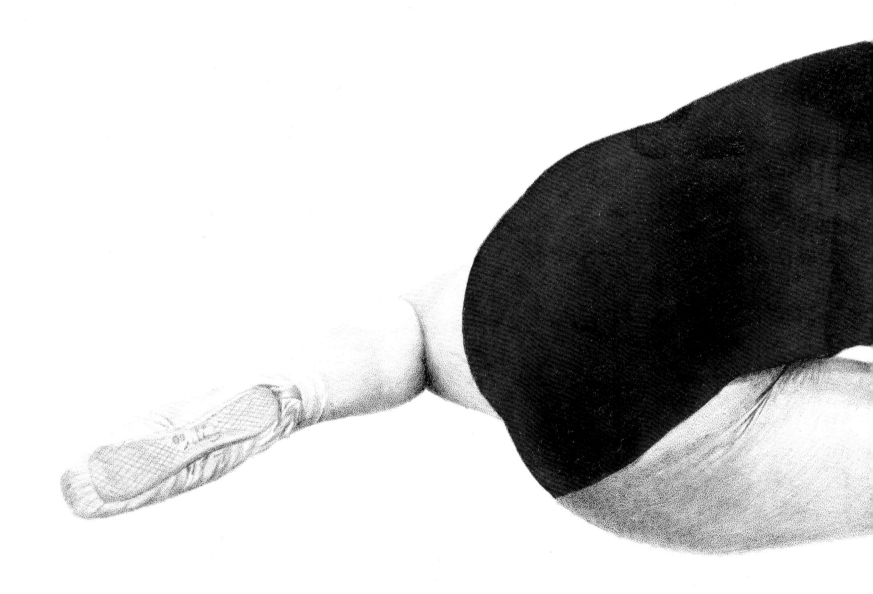

A REIDMORE

BOOK

© 1981 Len & Betty Gibbs

Canadian Cataloguing in Publication Data

Gibbs, Betty
The Art of Len Gibbs
ISBN 0-919091-03-2

1. Gibbs, Len. I. Gibbs, Len. II. Title.
N6549.G52A41981 760'.092'4 C81-091296-1

A Reidmore Book

Distributed in Canada by McClelland & Stewart Limited

.

Design & Editorial	Randy Morse
Typesetting & Design	Hallis Graphics Ltd.
Separations	Color Graphics Ltd.
Production	Van Campenhout Productions Ltd.

Printed and bound in the U.S.A.

DEDICATION

For Brandy and Mike

ACKNOWLEDGEMENTS

The production of this book has brought together the help of many friends and the talent of many experts. For all of their assistance we extend our appreciation.

We must offer a special thanks to all the people who allowed their paintings to be photographed and to the many photographers across the country who responded to our request for assistance. We are particularly indebted to Rob d'Estrube, who used his special skills to take more than half of the color transparencies used in this book.

We are also grateful for all the models who posed willingly and patiently. Though they sometimes suffered inconvenience, they gave graciously of their time and help.

For his expertise in preparing color separations, and in employing the art of the color analyst, we wish to thank Wayne Brinker for his help.

And finally, to Marianne Morse who helped with typing and editing, and Randy Morse who had the idea for this book in the first place, and bore most of the burden of its production, our thanks for your encouragement and friendship.

L. & B. G.

LEN GIBBS *by Dorothy Oxborough*
oil pastel 6" x 5"

INTRODUCTION

I first met Len and Betty Gibbs in the fall of 1978, when as Director of the Mendel Art Gallery in Saskatoon, I was the recipient of a Canada Council Director's Purchase Grant. I had decided to use the grant to strengthen the Gallery's holdings of Canadian realists, and the work of Len Gibbs had been highly recommended.

After thirty-five years of close association with art, both as a painter and as an arts administrator, I must admit to being still somewhat shy of artists. I feel the term "artist" is not something that one adopts oneself, but is rather an adjective applied by others. It is an honor earned. It is recognition.

As a breed, artists tend to be self-made men and women. People with a strong sense of conviction, direction and purpose; people with strongly-held philosophies and opinions about themselves, their work and the work of others. Yet most remain sensitive, gentle individuals, preferring personal anonymity, leaving their creations to speak for them. For these reasons, meeting artists to discuss their work can, at times, be a trying experience.

Needless to say, with little to go on but the recommendation of others, I was in a somewhat apprehensive state of mind when I rang the bell of the Gibbs residence in Oak Bay. Len's output was limited, little had been written about him, and his work was quickly snapped up by private collectors. He was, for me in 1978, a virtually unknown quantity.

I had arranged for a thirty-minute appointment. I stayed four-and-a-half hours.

Betty Gibbs proved to be a charming, witty lady of absolute sophistication, rather than the "dragon lady" she was rumored to be, in defense of Len and their personal privacy.

Len was relaxed, and grew more so as we talked freely and with common accord, his manner in marked contrast with the bristly, super-charged, frosty-red pirate image he was known to project.

In the broad "gallery" (there is no other word to describe it) which leads from the foyer to the living room of their home, hung works by artists whom Len and Betty respect. Though broad in scope and style, these works had one thing in common; they were all highly original in both concept and execution.

Entering the living room, my attention was immediately drawn to a panel painting sitting on an easel in one corner. I was struck by the craftsmanship of the work. Its locale reminded me of the rolling rangeland of southern Alberta, where prairie finally gives way to the foothills of the great ranges of the Rockies. A young woman in well-worn jeans was quickly gathering washing in advance of an oncoming storm; *Monday Thunder*.

I quickly purchased the work for my gallery. Betty sighed. She had lost the only original Len Gibbs currently in their home — once again!

Because of their preoccupation with creating images, few artists think of either writing a book, or of someday having a book written about them. I am sure this is true of Len Gibbs. Yet somehow, sitting in his living room and realizing that *Monday Thunder* would be only one of a handful of his works in a public collection, it did seem a shame that more people could not have access to his work. As I now write this introduction to his first book, it seems inevitable and right that this publication should come about, for it will do much to alleviate that need. There can be only one original work. For an artist as popular as Len, reproduction in book form allows for the larger audience his work deserves.

This publication brings together the talents of both husband and wife in a manner that serves as an introduction to their life with art. A rare and compellingly unique experience. Both Len and Betty are artists in their own right, Len of course as a painter, Betty as a writer. Together they have crafted a book that is remarkably honest.

In a series of crisp vignettes, Betty describes Len's art as the catalyst that has placed them individually and as a family firmly in a world of human experience that all can share and delight in. Through her use of quotes, Len emerges as the artist whose company I enjoyed on that first visit. A very sensitive and gentle man, whose strongest statements could only be made through his paintings and drawings, or through Betty's pen.

This book however, is chiefly about the *art* of Len Gibbs, a realist in life as well as art. His camera is a tool of his craft as much as is his impeccable draughtsmanship, using both to create such a depth of field as to almost approach the surreal. His technical mastery of the acrylic medium, which he uses in a manner reminiscent of egg tempera, leaves nothing to accident. His tightly drawn images interweave themselves into a wholistic tapestry of design. Like a miniaturist, each of his brush strokes is interdependent upon the other, each texture seeks balance and every inch of panel is drawn in to compliment and be an integral part of the subject. Each statement begins with a broad underlying armature, an abstract plan to which all else is hung. The original theme is never forgotten. As a result, Len's compositions always work, regardless of the scope of his total statement. The complexity of detail, when studied, gives both the joy of discovery and adds "vocabulary" to Gibbs' own comment.

I write to introduce a book. Betty writes to introduce Len, and in so doing, to herself, their family and something of their life together. Len in turn introduces the viewer to life, to his reality, to moments of human emotion, concern, escape, joy and performance. He places in each of his works an element of nature, of life itself. His paintings represent an introduction to topics that may be discussed at great length, and in great depth, through subject matter seemingly mundane — or at least "normal."

I invite you to enjoy Len's first book. I am sure it will whet your appetite for more of this superb western realist's work.

John Climer
Victoria, 1981

THE MUSICIAN
acrylic 20½" x 32"

COFFEE BREAK

acrylic 13" x 18"

ON ART

Len Gibbs was born in Cranbrook, British Columbia, in 1929. When he was five his father died and the family moved to Brandon, Manitoba, to be close to his maternal grandparents. He went to school there, and later in Edmonton, where most of his teachers did their best to discourage a career in art. It was not until he joined the Navy, at seventeen, that he took his first and formal art training. To fill in the long hours between watches, he signed up for a correspondence course in art and worked on the lessons in the quietest place on the ship: the torpedo room.

"The Gibbs family motto," he says, "is *Frapper au but,* which I have always translated as meaning *Get off your butt.* You don't gain anything by sitting around dreaming. You have to get moving and work.

"I spent seven years studying anatomy — bones, muscles, proportion, structure. I have no patience with today's general attitude toward teaching fine art which seems to be: *don't damage his creativity!* Serious artists must master difficult techniques — only then can they be free to express themselves. It's a freedom that can only be gained as a result of self-discipline — long, lonely hours of learning how to draw, of learning perspective, anatomy, color — a dozen different skills that may finally come together to make a competent artist. Creative success comes only from mastering basic techniques and knowledge, not from the easy, self-indulgent attitude that so many of today's aspiring artists seem to have.

"After all, you don't give a kid a piano and say: *bang away on that for three or four years, and you'll be another Beethoven.* First he has to learn harmony, theory, fingering and how to play scales — he has to master the basics.

"A country needs to feed the hearts and spirits of its people. In any of the arts, only an artist who has learned his craft well has anything to say.

"Art schools take in thousands of students every year and yet we don't seem to be graduating any competent artists. It is a great tragedy that these youngsters give up art in frustration, simply because they haven't been taught the basic skills and can't transfer their creativity to canvas."

WARMING UP
acrylic 15" x 24"

ON MARRIAGE

About the time that Len and I were getting married, in 1953, a new book came out called *I Married An Artist*. It was displayed for weeks in a bookstore that I used to pass on my way to work. The cover illustration showed a young lady sitting on a stool, head buried in her hands and obviously crying her heart out. I don't know who wrote the book. I know I didn't read it.

Artists have an undeserved reputation for being unreliable and a thoroughly bad lot, so though the book's cover illustration could have been used just as appropriately for a volume titled *I Married an Insurance Actuary*, it may not have sold as many copies.

We know a lot of artists. All of them are still married to their first spouse. All of them have raised nice families. All of them are honest, hard-working and reliable. Their emotions may be a little closer to the surface than most, they may see a more acute image of the world, but perhaps that is why their minds are so quick and their conversation so amusing.

Len and I enjoy each other's company. For all but a few of our twenty-eight years as a couple, we have spent twenty-four hours a day together. I have friends who wonder how I can stand having my husband home every day. I wouldn't have it any other way. Len's studio is upstairs, my office is on the main floor. I keep the books, look after correspondence, make cups of tea, fill in government forms, do a little free-lance writing and answer the phone.

Telephones are a necessary evil in our life; we both dislike them. Len works with acrylic paint and the little puddles of color that he mixes dry up so quickly that to be interrupted for even a short phone call often means that he has to paint an entire area again. This is particularly true when he's painting skin tones, so on days when I know he's painting a face, nobody gets through to him.

Early in the year, he likes to get his committments organized. There will be so many paintings for this gallery, so many for another. The numbers are small, as he can only paint about twenty finished acrylics in a year. These, along with a few watercolors and dry brush works are all he can do.

At least, that's the theory.

In practice, it seldom works out that way. Len is a softie and hates to say no to nice people. When a gallery phones and wants an extra painting for some special reason, even though it means he will have to work nights and on weekends, they can usually persuade him to do it. They can, that is, if they get through to Len. We joke that the word in the gallery world is they can get a painting if they talk to Len. If they talk to me, "the dragon lady," they haven't a prayer.

Nobody quite believes that an artist doesn't have a dozen or so finished canvases stacked against the wall. We get a lot of phone calls from people who would like to come over to select a painting right from the studio. This is nice and rather flattering. Usually even though we can't sell them a painting, we invite them over. Some have turned into very dear friends.

Almost as soon as Len finishes a painting, it is crated and sent to a gallery. I don't have a painting myself. Once, to shame him, I ordered a nice frame and hung it, empty, over the living room mantle. When he needed a picture in a hurry for a special exhibition, he painted it to fit my frame and shipped it off without a moment of remorse. We have an Adrian Dingle over the mantle, so things could be worse. Still, I'd rather have a Gibbs.

SAND CASTLES
acrylic 16" x 21"

SAND CASTLES II
acrylic 15" x 28"

AT THE OLD WAREHOUSE
acrylic 17" x 24"

THE BUILDER

acrylic 17" x 25"

ON ONE-MAN SHOWS

Children are such conformists! When Len first left his job to stay home and paint all day, our children at first were a little embarrassed. All the other dads in the neighborhood went off to work in the morning and came home at night. Their dad was an outsider in the daytime suburban world that had always been monopolized by mothers and children.

Not that the neighborhood saw much of him. A major gallery had offered him a one-man show and it took most of his waking hours to paint the pictures for it. With what Len still describes with amusement as an indication of my great faith in him, I went out and got a *real* job. I worked for the first year until the show was painted and successful.

There followed a succession of one-man shows. Galleries love them. They create a good deal of excitement and bring a lot of people into a gallery.

Len however has always disliked one-man shows; every time he has one he swears he will never do it again.

Most artists we know hate them. For one thing, they have to paint for months without any income. As the paintings lie around the studio they begin to have doubts about them. They study them too closely, and begin to think they could have done them better...or differently...or perhaps they shouldn't have done them at all...and eventually they think that if they had the time, they would throw them all in the fire and start over.

They worry that past achievements are indeed past, that this time no one will come to the show, no one will buy a painting, that they will be reduced to spending their declining years selling pencils on street corners.

COLORING
acrylic 16″ x 24″

ON SAILING

Apart from his own totally undistinguished career in the Navy, Len seems to cherish a belief that somewhere in the family was an old sea-dog. He wears a Greek fisherman's cap, rubber deck-boots and blue jeans, which he calls *dungarees.*

He once met a very young lady who thought he was a pirate. It was apparently his moustache that gave him away, but he was pleased to be mistaken for a true-blue salt. He swashed and buckled around for days.

He and a couple of chums sail together. For these expeditions Len appoints himself cook and plans elaborate menus that would not disgrace a first-class restaurant. Mostly though, they seem to dine on bologna sandwiches because the stove wouldn't work, or they ran out of propane, or the weather was too rough.

In one particularly perverse boat they have been fog-bound in shipping channels, stuck in the mud off Spanish Banks and becalmed and drifting when the engines quit. Indeed, they have been rescued so often that when they aren't in trouble they worry that the Coast Guard will think they are giving their business to someone else.

On one misadventurous voyage, the fan belt on the engine broke and they drifted helplessly into the path of an oncoming freighter. The story varies about how close the larger ship actually came, but as they looked up at a wall of rusty steel towering over them, one of them came up with the handy hint that a good emergency fan belt could be made with a pair of pantyhose. It wasn't a very helpful suggestion at the

time, since none of the three happened to have a pair along. Len however now keeps a pair in his sailing bag, and claims his wife understands.

WATER PAIL *acrylic 16" x 24"*

WIND FROM THE SEA
acrylic 17" x 24"

LINE SQUALL
acrylic 15" x 24"

MINNOWS
acrylic 18" x 24"

ROCKY SHORE
acrylic 15" x 27"

L. GIBBS

TYING ON THE LURE
dry brush 16" x 13"

ON ROOTS

Although we now live on the west coast and love to be by the sea and sail on it, Len doesn't often paint coastal scenes.He was brought up on the wide expanse of the western plains and still feels most at home there.

"I think," he says, "that where you spend your childhood sort of gets into your soul. The colors, the moods, the shades of tone at different times of day offer new revelations every time you look, and they become a part of you when you are young. You could be away from the place of your upbringing for fifty years and go back and still feel that you have come home.

"Once we went to the smallest Baleric Island, Menorca. I visualized the carefree life of an artist in a Mediterranean villa. We arrived late at night. All we could see out of our hotel window was a big, black void. When it got light, we could see that the void was the Mediterranean Sea. Everything was red, white and blue — blue ocean, white buildings, red tile roofs. Stunningly beautiful, and of course absolutely impossible for me to deal with as an artist.

"We kicked around the idea of moving to Ireland. They cherish their creative people — writers, composers and artists don't pay any income tax. That part of the deal was certainly appealing. I even think I could paint that troubled land, but I could never feel at home there. After about a month I'd need to come back to familiar landscapes and familiar ways of life."

SHOEING
acrylic 17" x 20½"

DECEMBER DUSK
acrylic 16" x 27"

ON FORTS & STARSHIPS

"A few old boards, a rag on the end of a stick; to John it was a castle with banners and pennants flying over knights in shining armor...a log fort to withstand the attack of heroic savages...a starship piloted by astronauts, outwitting strange creatures from outer space.

"Children's imaginations are beautiful and terribly fragile. Unfortunately, by the time they reach grade four, they have usually had their creativity stifled in efforts to make them conform.

"John's mother is a friend of ours. When we went to see her one day, I noticed the fort John had built by the fence. There were all sorts of soldiers and dragons scattered around, and I thought I could do a couple of paintings of him.

"I considered how I was going to approach the paintings, and decided I'd like one painting of him building a model spaceship. I decided on an indoor setting, with an 'after supper' lighting; the room mostly in darkness with a strong light on the boy's face.

"I bought a model kit and dropped it off to him after school. I asked him not to start building it until I phoned, as I didn't want him to have it finished before I got back that evening. After dinner, I phoned and told him to go ahead. He had been anxious to get started, and had all the pieces sorted out, so that, even though he lives only a few blocks away, by the time I got there he had almost finished putting it together.

"The next day I got him to pose for me outside by his fort. In his haste to get the model together the night before, some of the pieces were not very straight, and as he 'flew' it some of the parts fell off. John didn't mind; they were easy to glue back on.

"I worked with him a long time to get the pose just right. Eventually the fort was in deep shadow, so I had to move him out onto the lawn to get the lighting I wanted.

"I hate to bother people and ask them to pose for the same painting over and over again, just because I can't get it right. It was getting dark by the time I finished working with John, but happily I finally had enough material to go ahead with the painting."

NEW MODEL
acrylic 16" x 23"

SPACEPORT
acrylic 17½" x 24"

ON TASTE

"Most people don't have a familiar vocabulary about art. They read the jargon that academics write about it, or they hear verbose curators expounding their views and they don't understand what they are talking about.

"Frankly," says Gibbs, "I'm with them. I don't know what these experts are talking about either. They go out of their way to make a very simple subject sound very complex, and it has the effect of making people very nervous about art and very unsure of their own taste in it. They apologize with the old phrase, *I don't know anything about art but I know what I like.* If they have looked carefully at enough art to know what they like, then they do know something about art. Taste in clothes, furniture, cars or art, is a very personal thing. Certainly, quality is important, but if you like it, you shouldn't have to explain why to anyone.

ON INDEPENDENCE

Though city-bred, Len — like so many other realist painters — has chosen to live away from the major cities. He has never applied for a government grant as he feels that artists shouldn't become "welfare bums." Nor has he joined or accepted membership in any official art groups.

"I'm an independent artist and a capitalist. I'll make it on my own. I have no patience with mediocre talents that band together like a bunch of marauding vigilantes and then try to infringe on the freedom of others. It's too much like a union. No one tells me what to paint or when to paint or how to paint it."

HOP SCOTCH
acrylic 16" x 24"

ON DRAWING

Instruction in the style of art Len wanted to pursue simply wasn't available — so he taught himself.

"Looking back, I think I set up a very good, practical, academic art course for myself. I bought books and borrowed from the library. I studied old masters and new masters and spent a lot of time just drawing in pencil and charcoal before I ever got into color work.

"I drew thousands of arms and legs without skin, so I could see what each muscle was doing. I put them in different positions and drew them again. Then I colored each muscle in a separate color, so I could follow how it moved in a new position. I used to know the names of all the muscles.

"I drew pages and pages of eyes and ears and noses. I drew spheres and pyramids, burlap, rubber boots, glass, metal, diamonds, just so I could learn to draw different textures.

"I drew skeletons and then added muscles and skin. I still go back to the skeleton if I'm working out some tricky anatomy. I spent most of my spare time for seven years drawing everything and anything.

"Recently I met an academic type who admired my color and composition. *But what a pity,* he muttered, *that you ever learned to draw.*

"Well, you can't win them all!"

ON SKETCHING THE PRAIRIES

"Many times a year I go back to the prairies for a sketching trip. It's enormous country, with people and buildings scattered very thinly over a vast landscape. It holds an awesome beauty that I find emotional and intense."

Before he leaves on a prairie sketching trip, Len always finishes the painting he has on his easel. He cannot leave a half-finished painting and then come back to it five or six days later. By then he will have lost the "feel" of it, the mood of what he was trying to say.

His sketching trips are leisurely treasure hunts along the backroads. Here he finds the unmelted remains of snowdrifts, follows the wandering tracks of horses as they graze in a pasture, sketches a boy climbing over a fence or a pond locked in ice, dogs, farmers and weathered utensils. Compositions that most of us would never see, offer themselves readily to him. From April leaves to the snow-streaked hills of December, his art is rooted in the particular landscape that he calls home.

ON "MONDAY THUNDER"

Everywhere Len goes, he sketches scenes and records details on film. Over the years he has built up huge reference files and sometimes feels like a theatrical set designer as he takes a tree from here, a fence from there, a horse from another location and assembles them in one painting. All elements in his paintings actually exist someplace, but seldom does he find everything so well-arranged in one location that it pleases his eye exactly as it is.

In the preliminary sketches for *Monday Thunder*, Len tried several different backgrounds from his files of old buildings before deciding that a building simply wasn't necessary in the composition. In the final sketch, he used rolling country and a stormy sky as background elements with the isolated, almost full-length figure set to one side.

He waited for a windy day to study the effect of clothes blowing on a line. When our daughter came home for the weekend, he had her pose in the garden, reaching up to take clothes from an imaginary clothes-line.

Our son and daughter have been pressed into service as models for years. They are both grown now and still turn up in paintings looking like young ranchers or farmers' wives. Len says, laughingly, that he likes using them as models because "the price is right." The truth is that they have been posing for him for so long that they understand quickly what he wants them to do and are easy and natural to work with.

MONDAY THUNDER
acrylic 16" x 24"

ON PAINTINGS-THAT-NEVER-WILL-BE

There are two paintings that nag Len. The ideas for them keep surfacing, but they will likely never be done.

The first is a Spring painting, where the grass is sprigged with dandelions and the grey fuzz on purple crocuses. He wants to paint a Hutterite lady in her long, flower-spangled skirt, feeding her chickens.

The other is a Winter painting, done on a day when one can hardly tell where the snow ends and the sky begins; bare trees are dark against the snow, and a whispering wind breathes over the drifts. The stark black and white of the landscape sparked Len's imagination and in his mind he framed a picture of a Hutterite man, black beard and black clothes, working in the black and white land.

I wrote to a Hutterite colony but received no reply. Eventually Len phoned them.

"You will be welcome to come — but no pictures!," the man said firmly.

"But I wouldn't bother anyone," Len protested. "I would just take photographs or make quick drawings as you go about your regular work."

"You are welcome to visit at any time. But no pictures."

Not one to believe that such a refusal was really final, Len loaded his sketchbooks and cameras into the car and drove to the colony.

The welcome was both courteous and friendly, but...

"Please, leave your paints and camera in the car."

"I know," said Len. "No pictures."

But the paintings that might have been still come back to haunt him.

ON RODEO COWBOYS

Len is always on the lookout for good models. Almost every weekend during the hot prairie summer, in some small town, there is a rodeo. In dusty little fields in Bassano or Trochu, or in the show-business glitter of the Calgary Stampede, cowboys gather from the backwater reaches of the West to test their luck and skill in roping, riding and bucking.

They come in horse trailers, pick-up trucks, campers and mobile homes — mostly mud-colored, battered vehicles bunched together behind the stock pens, where cowboys eat, sleep, repair their equipment and bend the truth a little with the stories of horses they have ridden.

To get close to the action, the small-town rodeos are best. Len of course wants to get close to the cowboys. Not to see them roping or riding, but getting ready for their brief moments in the arena: buckling their chaps, stretching stirrups, carrying saddles or just sitting on the corral fence studying every move of the animals in the ring.

At one country rodeo Len found a treasure-trove of tall, lank cowboys. He dodged around horses and steers for the best part of a day sketching and photographing the young men as they readied for the eight-second ride that would seem like an eternity, a ride that could bring glory, indignity or injury.

Of course, the cowboys at the rodeo are all young and wear their city clothes: clean jeans and fancy chaps, polished boots and special hats saved especially for these occasions — not the grizzled old horsemen Len was hoping to find. Still, he felt there was much of interest going on, and he recorded details as he felt there was a painting or two somewhere in the material he gathered.

As we were leaving, we walked along the fences and saw kids perched on the rails watching their fathers and big brothers in the arena. They were bathed in the hot, harsh afternoon light, and Len did detailed sketches and studies of the boys before the final compositions were made. From all the material he gathered that day he did two paintings, *Rodeo Watcher* and *The Brothers*.

RODEO WATCHER

acrylic 15" x 10"

BROTHERS
acrylic 19" x 21"

GEARING UP
acrylic 16" x 24"

ON PAINTING COWBOYS

I suppose every artist has favorite paintings that he would like to keep. For Len, such a work was *Ranch Hand.* For almost a year after it was completed, it remained unframed on an ornamental easel in our livingroom. When it was finally reproduced on a poster advertising an exhibition of his work, the painting was shipped out. At least, we had a poster to remind us of the painting.

For the initial drawings, Len posed the model astride a chair on the patio. The details of the saddle were from old reference material he had gathered at a rodeo. Because of its design and the rawhide wrapping on the saddle horn, it is known as a buckaroo saddle. Buckaroo is a cowboy bastardization of the Spanish *vaquero.* It is nowadays used to describe cowboys who love the traditions of the Old West, and act the part with old-styled, elaborate and expensive gear. Len

wonders if the cowboy who owned the saddle was left-handed, as the rope is on its left side.

Len has searched for good cowboy models for years, so it was surprising that the best model he found was right in his own backyard. For two summers, our son worked on a ranch and came home looking like the tall, lank, dusty and unshaven cowboy Len had been searching for.

The painting titled *Mike,* was painted in close and meticulous detail on a stark white background. After days of concentrated work, Len got a tiny fleck of paint on the white backdrop and thought he had ruined the painting. The fence in the background thus became a necessary afterthought to cover the speck of paint. When it was finished, Len liked the painting better with the addition. He felt it established a working ranch atomosphere.

SADDLING UP
dry brush 12" circular

RANCH HAND
acrylic 22" circular

LOADING DOCK
acrylic 15" x 24½"

MIKE
dry brush 16" x 12"

ON DENIM & GOBLINS

That famous, if somewhat over-exposed painting, *Blue Boy,* by Sir Thomas Gainsborough was something he did as a challenge. The art afficionados of his time claimed that a painting in which the dominant color was blue, could not be successful. Obviously Sir Thomas proved them wrong.

Len likes the blue range too. That's something he has in common with Gainsborough. He likes today's blue denims and finds they are a delight to paint. His denims range from Prussian to Cerilian blue; as sometimes jeans fade to a purplish color he occasionally adds a little red.

Cobalt blue is a harsh color which he uses very sparingly. There's an interesting story about how Cobalt got its name. It is made from a silvery-white metal that is extremely toxic and in the old days the miners who dug it out of the earth died at alarmingly early ages. They blamed these early deaths on the *Kobolds,* goblins who inhabited the inner-reaches of the mines. Eventually, the metal itself was known as *kobold,* and in time this was anglicized to Cobalt.

APRIL LACE
acrylic 17" x 24"

WAITING
dry brush 13" x 13"

WORK MATES
dry brush 10½″ x 18¾″

ON BALLOONS

One rodeo we visited had a midway with all the usual ferris wheels and hot dog stands. As everything is grist for his mill, Len stopped to get a few photographs of the carnival, "just in case" he ever needed the reference material.

The need arose about a year later, when he decided to do a painting of a little girl with a balloon. Actually, the picture had been conceived in his mind two or three years earlier, but it was just one of those ideas that he kept simmering on a back burner.

He was having some difficulty visualizing the composition. He doodled with it a few times and always rejected the ideas. Finally, the carnival background and the little girl with a balloon came together in an unusual composition, a narrowly vertical canvas, 31" x 13".

Len was pleased with the finished painting; he felt it was very pink and white and feminine.

"All the round shapes," he says, "make it a happy painting. There's the ferris wheel, the balloon, the sucker, the pattern of her dress, the lettering on the fence has an *O* in it, even the white shapes of her socks between the toes and the straps of her shoes are round.

"I discovered that a balloon is a very difficult object to paint. I did it three times before I got it right. First I had to paint the inside of the far side with the blue sky showing through. There are two sources of light in a balloon — the light that comes through from the back and the light that reflects on it from the front. Simple complexities!"

BALLOON
acrylic 31" x 13"

ON THE
SEVEN DAYS OF CHILDHOOD

Some part of every artist's work remains forever his own. It is something that grows out of his personality and the period in which he lives. All of Len's paintings of children are an evocative record of contemporary childhood. For the most part, they are calm works with a message of life's renewal through children. A message of hope from the past, into the future.

For more than a year, Len contemplated the idea of a series of paintings which he called *The Seven Days of Childhood.* A group of seven related paintings, he felt, would be interesting to do, but each painting would have to be strong enough to stand on its own. Before he began making even the most preliminary drawings he tried, and rejected, many ideas before he settled on the final seven compositions.

Some of the models were from a nearby kindergarten, one was from a ballet class and others were the children of friends.

"I sometimes get into trouble when I get children to pose," says Len. "Many of them have a brother or sister who get a little put-out if I don't ask them to model too."

The young sister of *Thursday's Child* (the artist who has far to go), didn't wait to be asked. As Len sketched, she was playing on the other side of the room. When he started photographing, she heard the camera click and ran over to stand, grinning, beside her brother. *We always have our picture taken together,* she announced.

"Our dog Taffy is another who doesn't wait to be invited. She is twelve years old and finds most children a little too rowdy for her liking. For some reason, though, she really took to the little girl who posed for *Monday's Child.* As I sketched the girl brushing her hair, Taffy kept snuggling up trying to lick her nose. As *Monday's Child is Fair of Face,* I felt that a kiss on the nose would be quite appropriate, so I included the dog in the painting.

"*Friday's Child* and the child that was born on Sunday, are seven-year-old twins; good friends but also great rivals. I knew if I painted one I would have to paint the other as well.

"The girl was an easy model. We went out to her grandfather's farm and he gave her a baby dove to hold. Her eyes were full of wonder as she held the tiny new life in her hands.

"Her twin brother on the other hand was an awkward, shy model. Since my paintings are not portraits, but capture moments, my models have to be able to act a bit, put themselves into the picture, ignore me, and get into the game of what I want them to do. This particular little boy just couldn't do that. I tried to get him to gather eggs in the chicken coop, but he walked along very stiffly, eyeing me suspiciously the whole time. I sketched him because he would have been disappointed if I hadn't, but he looked more like an ad in a catalogue than a real kid. I tried a dozen different ideas with him, but without luck. He just couldn't relax. As a last resort, I thought I could get him to pose as *Sunday's Child,* being wise and good as he read a book. It worked! The book captured his attention and he was able to forget about me."

Monday's child is fair of face

MONDAY'S CHILD
acrylic 10" x 14"

Tuesday's child is full of grace

TUESDAY'S CHILD
acrylic 10" x 14"

Wednesday's child is full of woe

WEDNESDAY'S CHILD
acrylic 10" x 14"

Thursday's child has far to go

THURSDAY'S CHILD
acrylic 10" x 14"

Friday's child is loving and giving

FRIDAY'S CHILD
acrylic 10" x 14"

Saturday's child works hard for a living

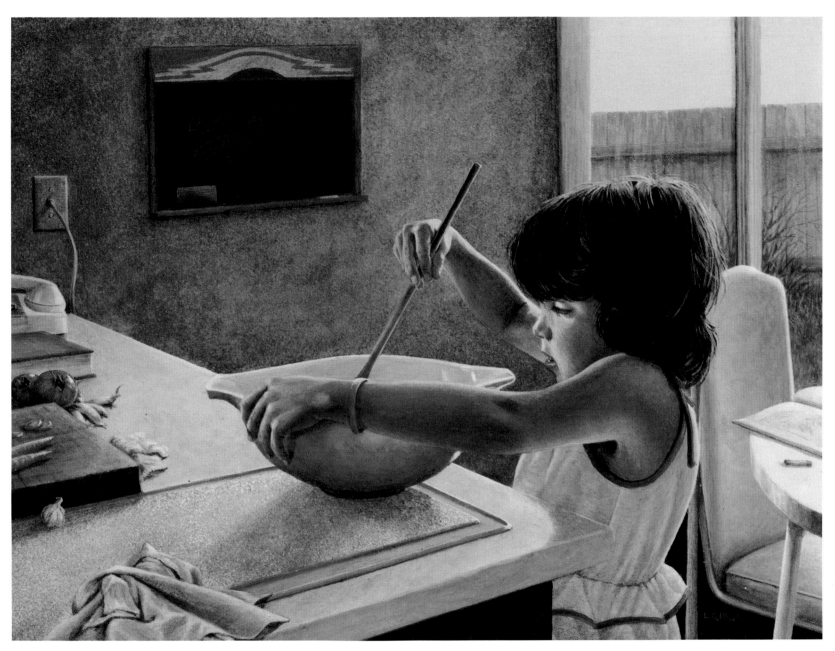

SATURDAY'S CHILD
acrylic 10" x 14"

But the child that's born on the Sabbath Day
Is fair and wise and good and gay

SUNDAY'S CHILD
acrylic 10" x 14"

ON PAINTING MOUNTIES

The black horses and scarlet tunics of the Royal Canadian Mounted Police are the symbols of Canada around the world. Today's Mounties are the followers of that first troop who little more than a hundred years ago, changed the course of history in Western Canada from the gun-slinging, whiskey-trading lawlessness that was spilling across the border from the United States to a territory safe for white settlers.

We arranged a meeting with the commanding officer of the RCMP Musical Ride when it was performing close to us, as Len wanted to do a painting of a modern Mountie.

We arrived at the location shortly after the horses and riders had arrived, and after inquiring at the local RCMP headquarters, found the horses stabled in the local arena.

It was black as midnight inside, but as our eyes adjusted to the light we could make out the shadowy forms of the big black horses tethered along the walls. Gradually, we began to discern that in the middle of the floor, sitting among bales of hay and bags of oats, were two young men wearing navy-blue coveralls.

"Hello there," said Len, in a loud and hearty voice. "Are you with the RCMP?"

"Yes, we are," one of the young men answered in a whisper.

Len whispered back, rather nervously: "What's the matter?"

"Nothing," came the soft reply. "We're baby sitting the horses and they're tired after the trip. We just try to keep it dark and quiet so they can rest."

Later, the commanding officer told us that on an overseas trip, the horses usually recover from jet-lag before the men do — but then perhaps the men are not as pampered.

A member of the Musical Ride must have at least two years in the regular RCMP before he is accepted into the equestrian course. Once accepted, he will spend almost a year learning horsemanship, riding, grooming and even a little veterinary training, as horses who travel so widely must have innoculations. Once in the Ride, a man will stay with it for two years. Four or five months of each year will be spent on tour throughout North America and Europe.

The horses are specially bred and start their training as three-year-olds. They are trained — not broken — we were told, so that they retain their spirit and character. They're parade-trained as well so that crowds, flash bulbs, bands and sudden noises don't make them skittish.

We were told a story about Bobby, a horse that served with the Ride for twenty-one years. He learned to accept being loaded into trucks and airplanes, remained calm through all manner of circumstances and noises — except one: bagpipes. They totally unnerved him. Many a rider lost his decorum as Bobby tried to put as much distance as possible between himself and that strange noise.

Then there was Lucky, well-trained but not one to suffer an indignity from man or beast. He would tolerate — once — a rider who jerked a bit too hard, but — twice — and Lucky would lower his head between his front legs and dump the rider into the dirt. Having suffered a kick or a bite from another horse, Lucky, in spite of the best efforts of his embarrassed rider, would move out of formation, wait as the line passed and deliver a well-aimed kick at the horse that had offended him. Then he would move calmly back into his place and continue with the business at hand.

We went to see the Ride perform in an open field. Freshly ploughed, it had been transformed into a slippery gumbo by a sudden downpour. The commanding officer took the men out to look at the conditions a couple of hours before the performance. As they got ready, grooming horses, polishing boots and bridles, there was tension in the air. The mud made the disaster of a spill a very real possibility, and with it the danger of injury to both horse and rider.

The Ride went well. No one slipped or fell. Back at the arena, there was a feeling of relief. As they took turns, quickly changing their red coats and walking the horses, the young constables laughed and chatted and lit up cigarettes.

Uniforms and equipment are kept in a large van and inside one of the doors we noticed a decal that had been glued up: "Happiness is owning your own horse." Someone had crossed the "s" out of "horse." The spelling may have been off, but the sentiment was clear. Red-blooded as well as red-coated, those young constables!

It is always a delight when someone first encountered in the course of business, later becomes a good friend. We still exchange Christmas cards with the commanding officer of the RCMP Musical Ride. He is one of those people we have to dinner every time he is in our part of the world.

STEEDS
acrylic 16" x 24"

ON SADDLEMAKING

The cowboy's saddle hasn't changed in a hundred years. It was big, so that on long cattle drives, the men on the night watch could doze in the saddle without falling off. It has a high cantle at the back to prevent the rider from slipping off if his horse decides to hunker down on its haunches when he ropes a steer. He can tie his rope to the saddlehorn so the horse can hold the steer while the cowboy does his work. Like new shoes, a new saddle needs breaking-in. The leather stretches, softens and begins to fit, the more the saddle is used.

On the outskirts of Calgary, we met an old saddlemaker padding and stitching heavy leather to a wooden form. He smoothed the intricate curves with his toil-thickened hands as he told an immigrant's story of fear and poverty in central Europe.

"This country best," he told us. "So free. If you were born here, you don't appreciate how free."

The massive immigration to North America from Europe in the early days of this century seldom was triggered by hope for a better life in a new land, but by famine, poverty and persecution at home. The first legacy of North America was hopelessness; in its early days it was a land populated by exiles. Against all odds, many of these people went on to build solid new lives in an alien environment. Some, like the saddlemaker, brought with them skills which, when they are gone, will be lost to North Americans forever.

HARNESS SHED
acrylic 18" x 24"

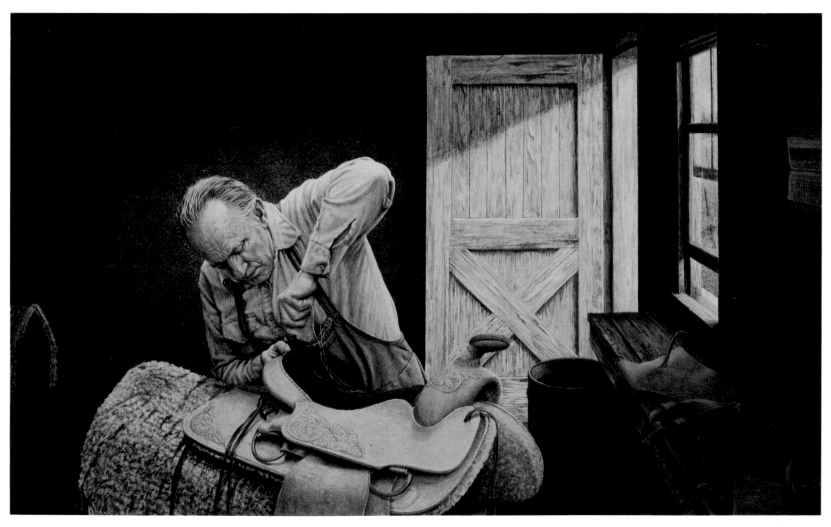

SADDLEMAKER

acrylic 17" x 24"

ON WORKING

Many people interested in art would like to visit an artist in his studio. To Len that would be like asking to visit him in the shower — an outlandish suggestion and an incredible invasion of privacy. He welcomes visitors to his home; often there is a finished painting on the easel in the livingroom. Sometimes, for very special friends, he will bring a painting down from his studio to show them, but he cannot and will not have anyone in his studio while he is working.

"In the first place," he says, "it's pretty dull to watch. I don't do flamboyant sweeps of color like a water-colorist or bash off a painting in a morning like someone working with a palette knife. People would fall asleep watching me. I use tiny sable brushes. Good ones, incidentally, are becoming increasingly difficult to find. I might spend a whole day just painting a hand that's half an inch long.

"In the second place I just can't go in for social performance of my work. With someone sitting by my elbow I would have to explain what I'm doing and I honestly can't explain it. I just do what I do because it looks right or feels right."

His studio is small enough to discourage lingering. The only chair is the one at his easel. Once a week the cleaning lady is allowed to vacuum the middle of the floor — but only the middle. On the floor and stacked against the walls are paper-stretchers, etching-plates, camera equipment, books, a weathered log, sketchbooks, and a pair of old boots that he intends to paint someday.

His bookshelves are orderly but the tops of tables, counters and filing cabinets are littered with sketches, photographs, pages from notebooks, paints, brushes and a bundle of long, dried grass. There's a cork wall with a yellowing list of painting ideas pinned on it, a few hasty thumbnail sketches in which he has worked out relationships of color, form and space, and usually an accurate pencil drawing of part of the painting he is currently working on. To see the metamorphosis of these doodles and drawings through to the finished painting is to follow the path of the brain from a hazy idea to the concrete fulfillment of a dream.

In the midst of the muddle, he tunes his radio to light classics and works bankers' hours from nine to five. Without permission, no one but me is allowed in the studio, and even I know better than to touch anything. It's chaos held together by dust — but he knows where everything is. Every few months, usually after he has completed a major project, everything is moved and cleaned, windows are washed, reference material filed, wastebaskets emptied, and order restored. It will stay that way for at least two days.

Once he is committed to a painting, he works at it until it is finished. He never abandons a painting to start on something new. He never works on three or four paintings at a time. His whole concentration is directed to the painting he is currently working on. That is not to say there are no unfinished paintings around. There are a few, but they have been permanently abandoned, rejects which for one reason or another, he feels have "no heart."

SEA WATCH
acrylic 16" x 24"

ON HOME

Our house was designed and built about seven years ago. Realizing that our children were almost grown and might soon be leaving home, we told our architect that we wanted "a cozy little cottage in which to spend our declining years." He, obviously, had no idea of how far we might be inclined to decline, for what appeared to be a "cozy little cottage" on the blueprints turned out to be a big, rambling place which we, the architect and the property tax assessor have finally agreed must be around two thousand square feet. It's hard to be sure as the house was planned to fit around large oak trees and rock outcroppings and is loosely S-shaped with a couple of appendages sticking out the sides. Len describes it as being shaped like a tadpole with water wings.

We had our first party here when the roof went on. We decorated an evergreen tree, nailed it to the roof and entertained the carpenters with wine and cheese while rain lashed through the window openings and we stood, shivering, among the two-by-fours and saw horses. A roof tree gives a blessing to a house, and it has been a good house ever since.

After we moved in, Len and I went through the place adding more than a mile of moldings — baseboards, wainscotting, a plate-rail in the dining-room. Len did the sawing and hammering and I followed up with a bucket of filler, patching up the cracks.

For the livingroom we rescued an ornate old mantel from a house that was being demolished, stripped off layers of pink, cream, green, mauve and red, then re-painted it a pristine white.

This is an old neighborhood so we wanted a brand-new, old-looking house that would fit in with its surroundings. We really know we've done everything right when people come in and think we've renovated an old home.

The house is decorated in soft blues, the same color as faded denim, and the straw yellows of prairie grass in August. There's a long, wide hall that leads from the front door to the livingroom at the back of the house. That, I think, was what sold us on the plan in the first place; the architect marked it "Gallery" on the blueprints. Now it's hung from ceiling to chair-rail with paintings and original prints. When we need to stretch our eyes after a long session of painting or writing, we can easily get outdoors to a huge deck off the kitchen, a little walled patio off the den or a plant-filled solarium off the livingroom.

Len's studio is shaped like a wide V. It's on the second floor. He also has a print room in the basement where he keeps his etching press and stores extra painting panels and watercolor board.

We remark, every once in a while, that the house is too big for us. But apart from one bedroom that is closed and empty, (children are inclined to take their furniture when they move away), we seem to use it all.

THE TRAVELER
acrylic 16" x 26"

ON CHOOSING SUBJECTS

To Len a painting has to come naturally. Many times friends have said, "I know a place that you would love to paint" or "I met a character who would be perfect for one of your paintings."

Len seldom follows up on these suggestions, because his response to an image is very personal. Deciding what he will paint in the first place is an intrinsic part of his work. There is something in his artist's eye that make some things paintable — and others not.

People sometimes contact Len to see if he will paint a portrait. The answer is invariably no. In the first place, the subject would not be his choice and he doesn't paint portraits as such. Any painting he does must stand on its own in a gallery and not merely please the family of the sitter. Besides, he likes to know his models and know that he can work with them. It is better to say no in the first place than disappoint the relatives later on.

Occasionally someone sends a few photographs, suggesting that Len work from those. That is something he won't even consider. It would not be his choice of subject, pose or lighting, nor would he feel comfortable taking any artistic liberties with the subject.

Though he often uses the children of friends as models, they are never offered an opportunity to purchase the painting. He usually gives the model an enlarged color photograph of the painting, but the art itself is always shipped to a gallery.

FETCHING POTATOES
acrylic 16" x 24"

ON PEELING POTATOES

I haven't been asked to pose often, and I am grateful. I'm one of those stiff, self-conscious people who don't make good models. Len once did a painting of me sitting by a window peeling potatoes. As he often does, he took it to a professional photographer to have it photographed so that we could have a permanent record of it. In due course, the photographer's bill arrived — but no photograph. I phoned to inquire. The photographer, whom I hadn't met, sounded about fourteen-years-old on the phone.

"Was that the painting," he asked, "of the old lady peeling potatoes?"

He had the grace to blush when I went to pick up the photo.

PEELING POTATOES
acrylic 21" x 17"

ON PAINTING BOXERS

"Athletes are a delight to paint. They're in good physical shape with no fat to hide what their muscles are doing. When I had a young boxer pose for *The Champion*, I wanted him to look hot and hard-working. Obviously, I was going to be fully occupied with drawing the subject, so I gave Betty a spray bottle of water to sustain the effect of sweat-soaked effort. She was a little uneasy about spraying that powerful-looking young man with cold water, but as she explained to him what she was going to do, she took the motherly approach: *Shut your eyes, dear...* I must say, he was very pleasant and patient about the proceedings. It is a painting that pleases me. Everything came down right."

THE CHAMPION
acrylic 24" x 24"

MARBLE PLAYERS
acrylic 16" x 28"

RECESS
acrylic 22" circular

ON THINGS NATIVE

Though magnificent landscapes and exotic ports are not Len's style, he does travel sometimes to remote corners to get material for a particular painting he wants to do.

We once flew to a remote Indian village, where the people of the community are still making snowshoes with traditional materials. We had met the manager of the factory in town. We phoned him the day before we left to tell him that we would be arriving, but didn't know what time we would be getting in.

"Don't worry about it," he replied, "I'll hear the plane coming in and drive out to get you."

Not exactly an international airport.

The ground was still frozen as we landed. A chill wind whispered along a windbreak of birch trees. The snow was patchy on the grass landing strip. The sky was a brilliantly intense blue.

There were no buildings of any kind at the airstrip. As the pilot tied down the plane and covered the engine with blankets, our friend rattled up in his pickup truck to take us to the factory.

Only one Native there spoke English; the rest spoke only Cree. The English-speaking boy had been appointed foreman and answered our questions as we looked around.

The workshop itself was built of peeled logs; a single room heated by a crackling, wood-burning stove. There was a shed off the room used for soaking and steaming strips of birch before they were clamped into the wooden jigs that would shape them. To cut hide into narrow strips, the native women pulled a pelt in a clockwise motion, around and around a sharp knife placed firmly in the table in front of them. Yards and yards of unbroken thonging were made from one piece of hide, then laced into the snowshoe with a series of intricate knots.

We also met an Indian lady who had taken over a trapline from her husband who had died some years earlier. She was large, efficient and warmhearted. Her little cabin was spotless. The main room was a combination livingroom, diningroom and kitchen with a worn linoleum floor and a scattering of wooden kitchen chairs. A small black coal and wood stove served for cooking as well as a source of heat.

As she bustled around making tea, she told us of the time, the previous winter, that she had shot a bear from her front door, and of the time that she had caught a raven who was killing her baby rabbits. She tied the raven up and scolded it. For three days she kept it, scolding it every time she passed it. Finally she let it go, but she felt she had won her point.

"He never came back again," she said.

In the Cree language, everything alive is personified. A tree or a flower is referred to as if it were a person, and yet the language has no words to define gender. This can lead to startling statements, such as our friend's remark: *That mother cat of mine, he's getting too fat!*

Cats and their kittens were allowed free run of the little cabin, but the dogs were kept strictly outside. Usually, the dogs were allowed to roam at will, but at the time of our visit, they were tied up; they too were accused of killing baby rabbits. When the rabbits were old enough to fend for themselves, the dogs would be let loose. In the meantime, each was housed in his own jerry-built shelter.

We walked with her as she went to feed the dogs. They all barked and bounced and wagged their tails. They seemed genuinely glad to see her. She spoke to all of them, bawled one of them out for once again spilling his water, but went to the stream to get more for him.

Len had to work quickly in the village, capturing scenes inside the snowshoe factory and outdoors along the shore of the snowcovered lake. In the back of our minds, we knew that the airplane could easily freeze-up in the biting north wind. We were anxious to get back to civilization before the short hours of daylight ended.

INDIAN DOG
acrylic 9" x 15½"

KUH-NAH
acrylic 24" x 22"

ON FOUR—LEGGED HUMANS

We once observed a cattle dog that was usually wary enough to stay out of pastures unless he was invited in to work. His high-spirited games of barking and chasing gophers irritated the horses and upset the cattle, and once had earned him a solid kick. At a word from his master, *Out!*, his game ended and he crept to the other side of the fence with a look of heartbroken disbelief.

One rider can't round up a herd, and that's when a dog becomes a welcome assistant. We watched the dog as he helped drive cattle to a new pasture, nipping at heels to keep them moving, darting across the field to bring back a wanderer, then back the other way to fetch a stubborn one who didn't want to move. He travelled six times as far as the cowboys and their horses, his pink tongue lolling out the side of his mouth, eyes bright as sequins as he crouched for a moment in the grass, calculating his next move.

He was a marvel; the cowboys couldn't have done their job without him.

I enthused about the dog. "Isn't he great! He just does everything right."

Oh he's pretty good all right, said his owner. *But sometimes he makes mistakes. After all, he's only human.*

OBEDIENT WATCHER
acrylic 16" x 24"

ON MIRROR IMAGES

Although it was a simple concept, *Mirror Mirror* offered many complications. In his preliminary sketches and drawings, Len foresaw some of the difficulties that he would face with the finished painting, which would have a variety of surfaces and textures.

With his drawing, *Saturday Night* and the preliminary watercolor for *Mirror Mirror*, he worked out many of the problems of composition and tone.

Originally he had thought that he would do the painting with a very dark background, but the more he thought of the concept the more he leaned toward a very light backdrop instead. The "white" wall on the finished canvas actually picks up all the colors used elsewhere in the painting. It has been built up with tiny flecks of the flesh tones, the browns and yellows of wood and hair, and the blue of the jeans. This coloring is all overlaid with transparent white but the "mother colors" sparkle through and hold everything together.

In most of Len's paintings the viewer can put himself into the picture, can become the kid flying the kite, the cowboy, or the little girl who has lost her ice cream cone. In this painting, because of the mirror, the viewer is definitely an outsider. There is no way anyone can become the girl in the painting. The viewer is looking at the scene from an entirely different angle than the figure in the work.

Len had our daughter pose for this, but without a mirror; it was almost an afterthought. When he started on the finished painting, he mentally turned her around and painted her face and hands in the mirror; as soon as he started on it, he knew that it was wrong. He asked her to pose again, this time with a mirror and realized immediately that, unless he was standing right behind her the reflection in the mirror couldn't possibly be a reverse image, so it was back to the drawingboard.

While the drawing *Saturday Night* is decidedly our daughter, Len didn't want to repeat the features in so closely related a painting. So, while there is a family resemblance, the face in the mirror was changed so as not to be a portrait.

AP ⅓   SATURDAY NIGHT

SATURDAY NIGHT
artist's proof 15½" x 7½" lithograph

MIRROR MIRROR (preliminary)
dry brush 10" x 12"

MIRROR MIRROR
acrylic 20" x 20"

ON PAINTING LOUISE

"I live in a west coast neighborhood called Oak Bay, a pseudo-English sort of place described as being behind the "Tweed Curtain." The favored style of dress here is mellowed Harris wool and comfortable shoes. The favorite drink is sherry, and the architecture a sort of "stock broker tudor." Indeed, it is said that the ladies of Oak Bay resemble the architecture, both being 'rather broad-beamed and generally half-plastered.'

"Louise Rose, my model for *Jazz Singer*, had bought her grand piano from a little old lady from Oak Bay who had stored it for a year or two in a somewhat leaky garage. Louise had to have the piano entirely rebuilt and set to the brilliant tone she likes best for nightclub work. The top had been badly spotted from rain coming through the roof. She had it refinished in ebony since no one could match the fruitwood color of the rest of the piano.

"I first encountered Louise quite by accident. Betty and I happened to have dinner where she was playing. She had such strength and warmth in her face that I wanted to paint her. When she took a break, I went and spoke to her about it. I must say she seemed pretty cool at first. I guess she gets a lot of yahoos talking to her. I insisted that I was sincere. Finally, she gave me her card and her agent's card and said: *Arrange it with my agent.* So I did.

"One of the terms that her agent insisted on was that if Louise Rose did not like the painting, I would destroy it.

"I don't know what I would have done if she had told me to throw it out. By the time I had finished it, I thought it was one of the most exciting paintings I had ever done — very strong and powerful.

"The painting was quite a challenge. It was the first time I had painted a colored person, and of course it was a totally new palette for me. The beautiful colors in the skin tones, bright reds and brilliant blues, just about knocked me out of my chair.

"I must have done a dozen preliminary color sketches before I started the finished painting. Louise's bone structure threw me a little at first. I had to go back to my anatomy books before I got it right.

"When I finally got into rendering the finished painting, I thought I could just slop some color onto the background and then mark the mirrors off with a ruling pen. That just didn't work. I ended up individually painting fifty-four little mirror tiles. Doing that very loose, abstract-looking background took five days.

"I started to worry that with all the busy little bits and pieces in the background, the figure itself would get lost. It doesn't. It stands out like a skyrocket!

"Happily, Louise Rose likes the finished painting; in fact, she became a little misty-eyed when she first saw it. She asked if she could reproduce it on the cover of her next record album, so I knew her enthusiasm went beyond mere acceptance.

"Since then, we have become good friends. Louise works in nightclubs five nights a week and teaches senior piano students in her spare time. She has been studying music since she was five. Once, on a dare, she joined the Philadelphia police force and was, as she says, *a damned good cop.* She was shot and wounded three times, mugged by a gang of prostitutes and set-up to be eliminated by drug dealers. She is an evangelist, a feminist, a musician and a great lady.

JAZZ SINGER
acrylic 16" x 24"

ON PAINTING JENNY

The model for these paintings was Jenny, daughter of the marine watercolorist Harry Heine. She chose the clothes she wanted to wear, an enormous hat dug out of a costume box in the basement, a sleeveless silver lame dress worn over a warm sweater because the weather was cool. With it she wore, at various times, gold slippers or sneakers when she grew tired of stumbling around on high heels. With great restraint she chose as her only accessory a rhinestone bracelet.

As her father is an artist, Jenny is aware of sketchbooks. The moment she saw the tools of the artist's trade, she became too precious. Little pinkies were sticking out in all directions and she tilted her head to various appealing and coy angles.

"I really had to sweat it with her," says Len, "and try to catch her at times when she was absorbed in her own thoughts."

For the major painting, *Jenny,* he composed the picture almost exactly as the scene had actually been with flowers and garden shrubs in the background.

"But," he says, "the whole thing looked staged. There were too many confusing elements of detail in it. To simplify it I changed the location so that she was sitting on an old clothesline stoop. There are two uprights on either side of the figure; one, the clothesline pole, and the other holding the box of clothespins. I debated a long time about where to place them, or whether to leave them out entirely. I really felt that the vertical divisions had to be there, but the placement was very important. As it is, I think the painting is all framed-in between the two uprights. Everything outside of them is only there to give the figure a little more space."

As always, the paintings show Len's skill in painting textures: satin and lace, weathered wood, grass, stucco and the knitted doll clothes are all carefully delineated. In another painting, *Parasol,*, the texture of the sunshade was accomplished with thousands of short, fine brush strokes interwoven with patient care.

JENNY'S DOLL
dry brush 10½" x 12"

PARASOL
acrylic 20" x 20"

JENNY
acrylic 18½" x 24"

ON GUNS

"Some paintings take a long period of creative gestation; they sort of linger in the back of your mind for years. You know it is something that you want to do, but the thoughts never quite jell. One such painting was *On the Mat*. The idea for the painting would surface occasionally, and I would doodle a few ideas on paper, but I could never quite get the powerful composition that I felt the subject demanded.

"Then, quite suddenly, the whole thing popped, full-blown, into my mind and I couldn't wait to get it on paper. The target is round, the eyepiece is round, the gun barrel is round — so the painting should be round, and the viewer should be looking right down the gun barrel.

"I lined up a model, a young man whose whole family enjoyed the sport of target shooting. Of course, with his years of training, he had been taught never to point a gun at anyone. As I stood working directly in front of him, he said, *Please, don't stand in front of the gun,* then moved the weapon slightly to the left. As I moved to keep in front of him, he reiterated, *Please, don't stand in front of the gun,* then moved the gun slightly to the right.

"I made him very nervous as I danced my little fandango trying to keep in front of the gun. Eventually I got what I wanted. I suppose because I had been kicking the idea around for so long, the actual rendering of the painting was easy.

"Because the viewer is the target, the marksman is looking right at you and his eyes follow you wherever you go. I think it's a disturbing painting, but then, guns are pretty disturbing anyway."

ON THE MAT
acrylic 22" circular

ON PAINTING THE CLERGY

It isn't often that Len changes the concept of a painting. He gets an idea, doodles a little sketch, then searches around to find the elements to make it all happen.

The missionaries were an important part of bringing civilization to the West and for this reason, Len wanted to do a painting of a priest. We contacted a mission. One of the Fathers there suggested an elderly priest who he thought would be happy to pose.

Len wanted to have the priest fishing from the banks of a river. Although he hadn't met the model, he did know that he was elderly. Rather than have the model stand for too long on the bank of the river in the chill Spring air, he decided to go and sketch the background material first.

We searched around until we found a suitable location. I "stood in" for the priest to give Len a sense of dimension in the scene.

With the background material well in hand, we went to meet the priest. As soon as we saw him, Len changed his mind about the painting. The priest had such a lovely face and manner that Len decided to abandon his initial plans and concentrate on the man himself.

The old gentleman was pleased to pose and as easy to work with and natural as a professional model. He fussed around to get everything just right. *Who would think,* he smiled, *that anyone would want to paint an old man like me.*

It was then back to the drawingboard, so to speak, to find a suitable background. Eventually, we found just the right church and again, I "stood in" for the priest.

QUIET MOMENT
acrylic 16" x 24½"

SISTERS
acrylic 20" x 20"